Coloring Book of Holiday Peace

Suzanna Stinnett

ISBN: 0692559420 Coloring Camelot
ISBN-13: 978-0692559420

Coloring Book of Holiday Peace

Welcome to a new collection of holiday scenes
including larger designs which are perfect for
the youngest coloring enthusiasts in the family.

Inside are two pages of each image for sharing or practicing.

Using ink?
The pages in the very back are for you to tear out and
use to protect the following page from
ink spots coming through.

The images are arranged
from the more complex to
the simpler through the book.

Any of these are fun for making your own wrapping paper as well!
The images toward the back are specially designed
to work as color-your-own wrapping paper.

Have fun coloring around the table together.

Peaceful wishes for your holiday season!

Suzanna Stinnett

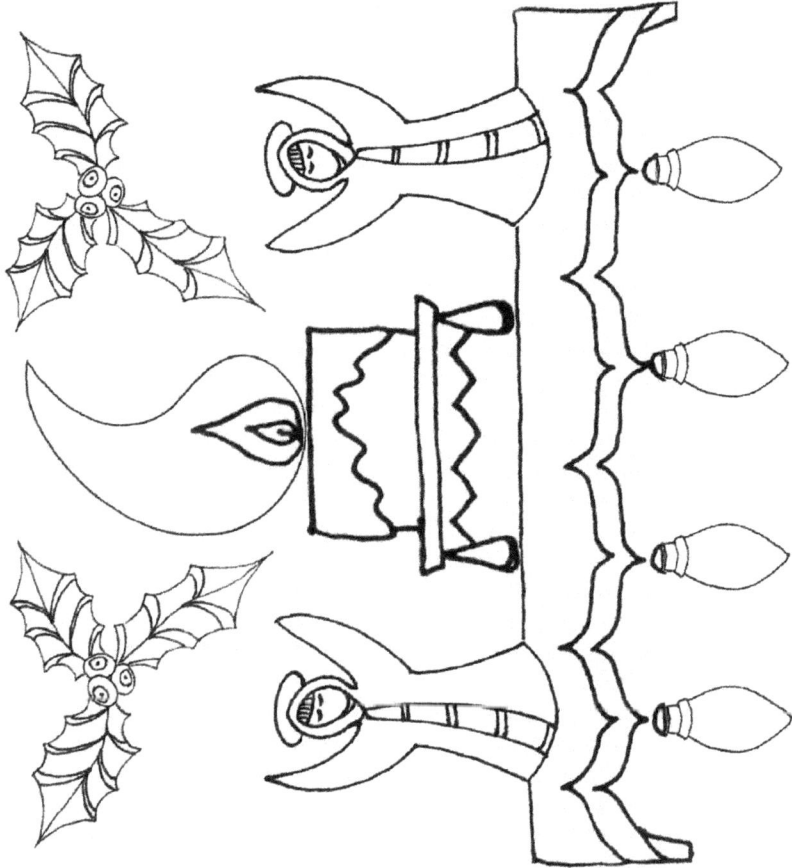

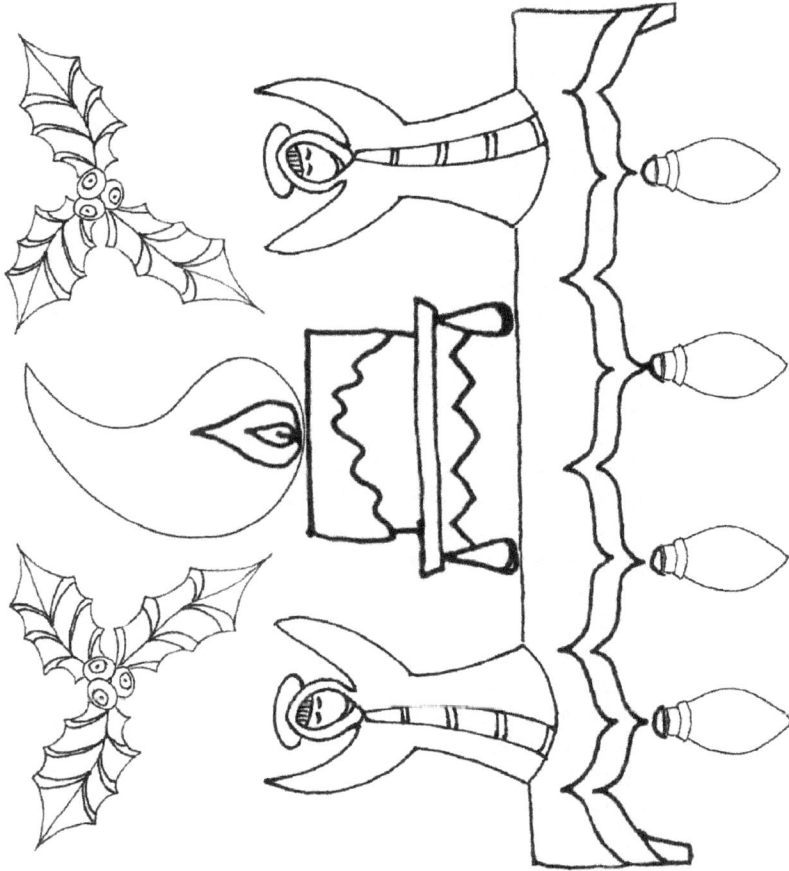

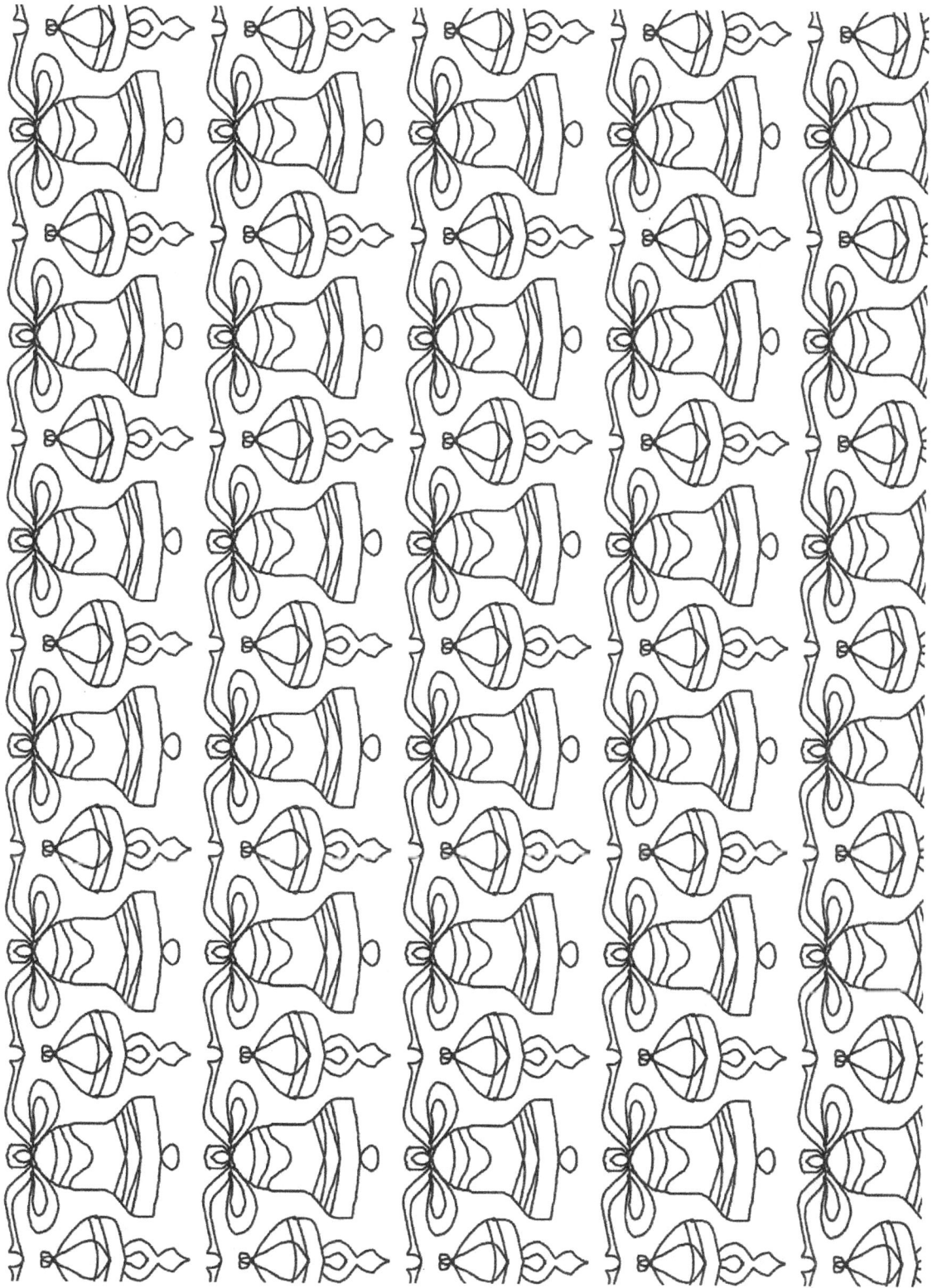

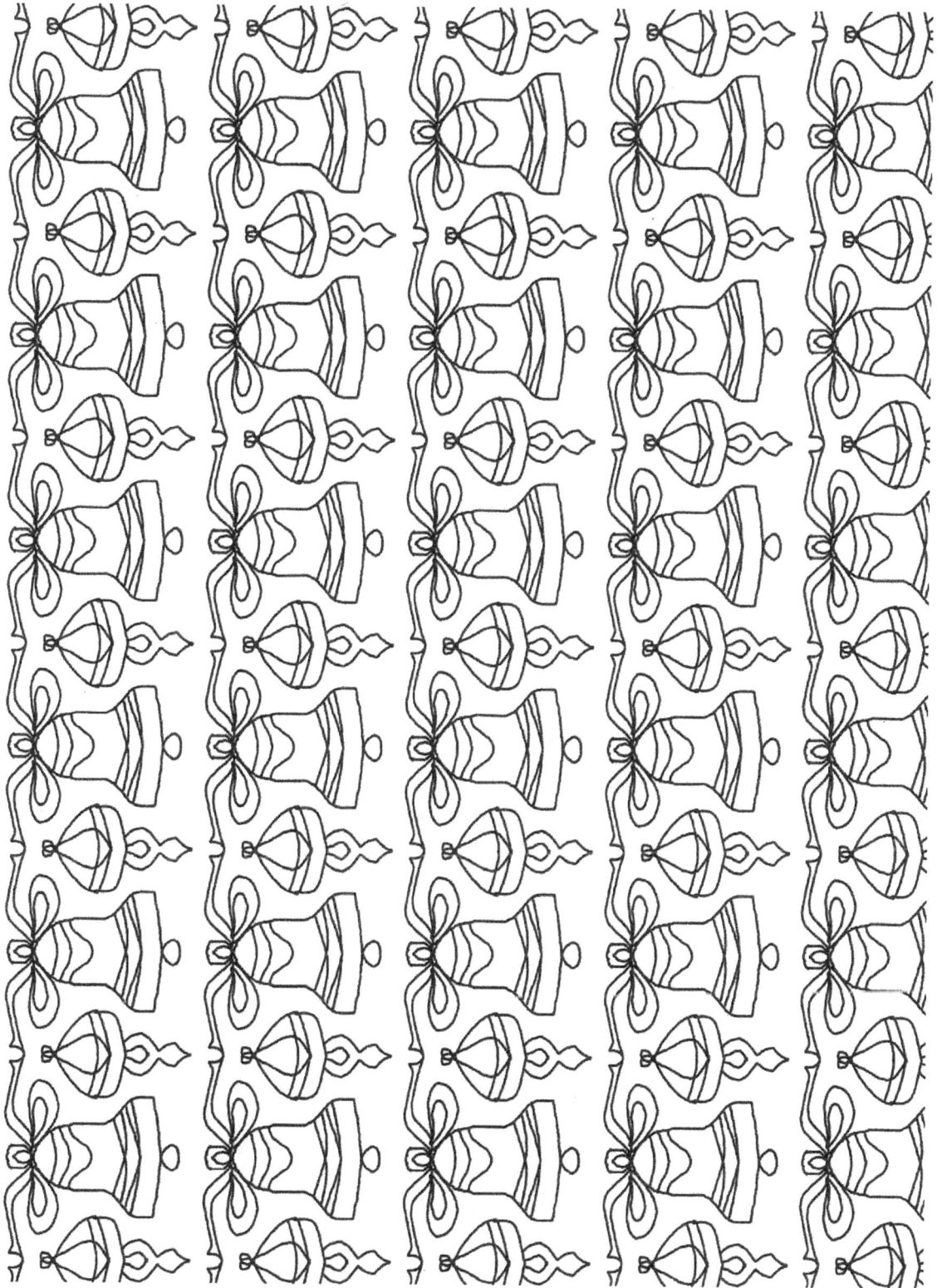

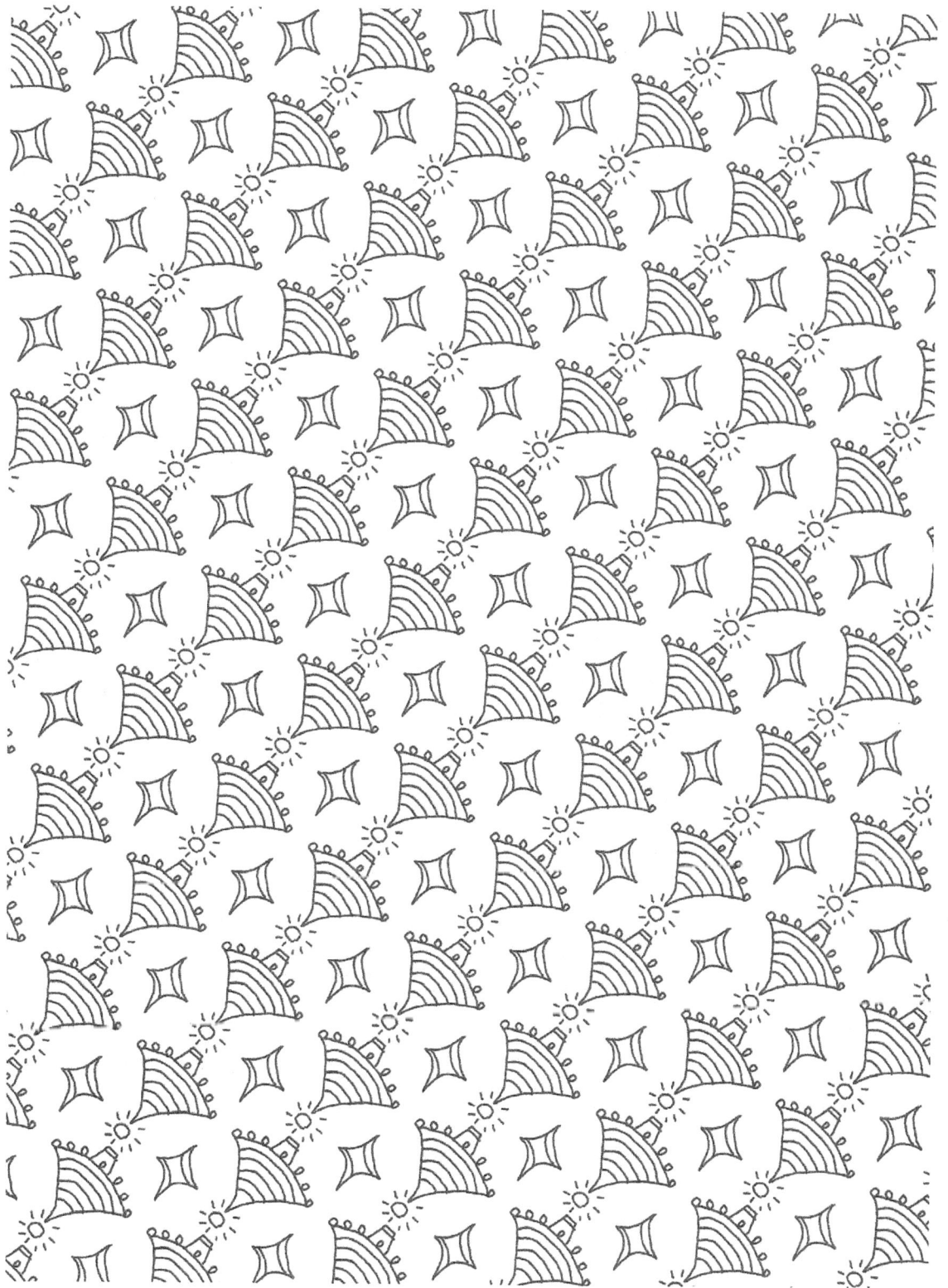

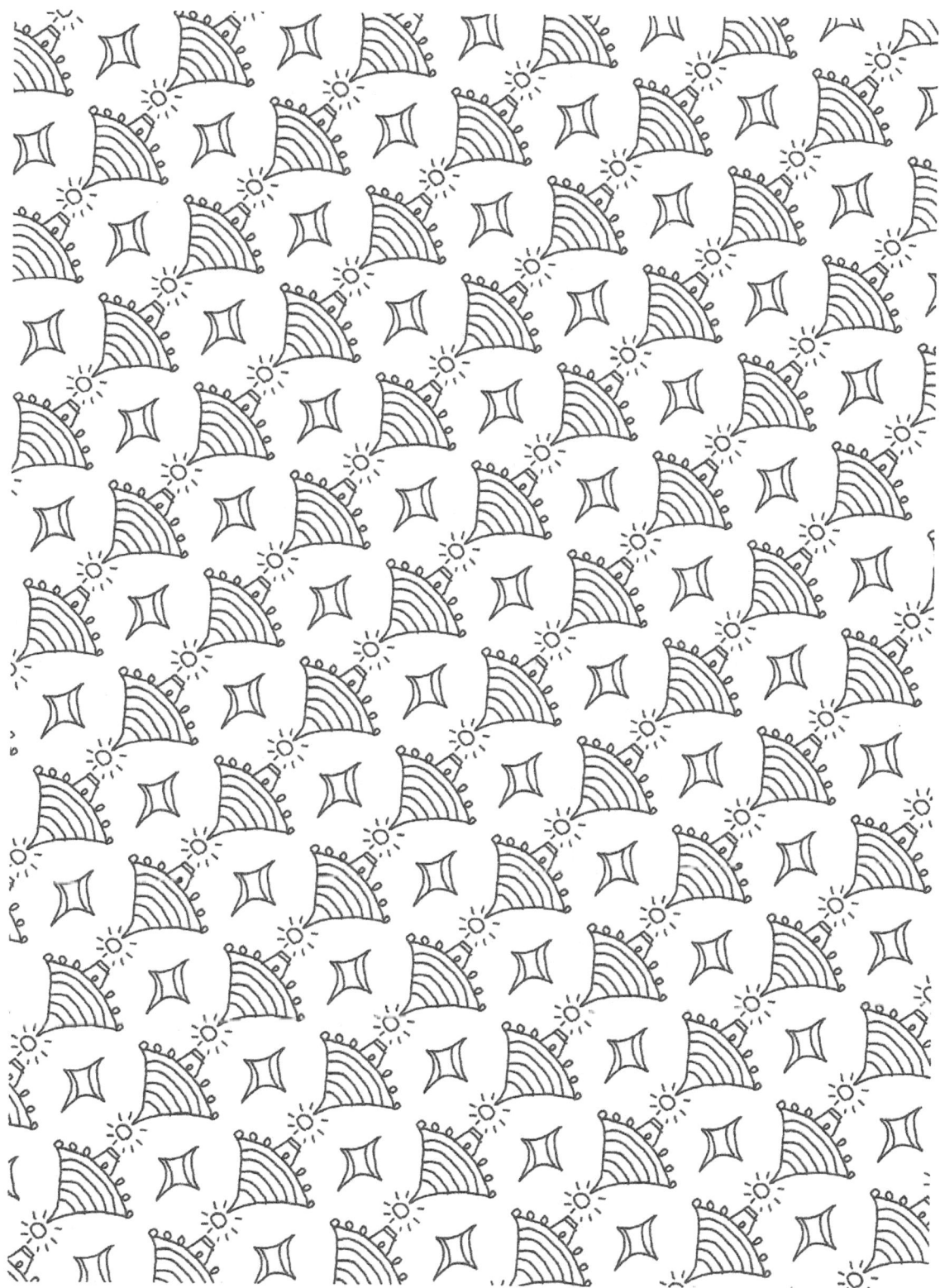

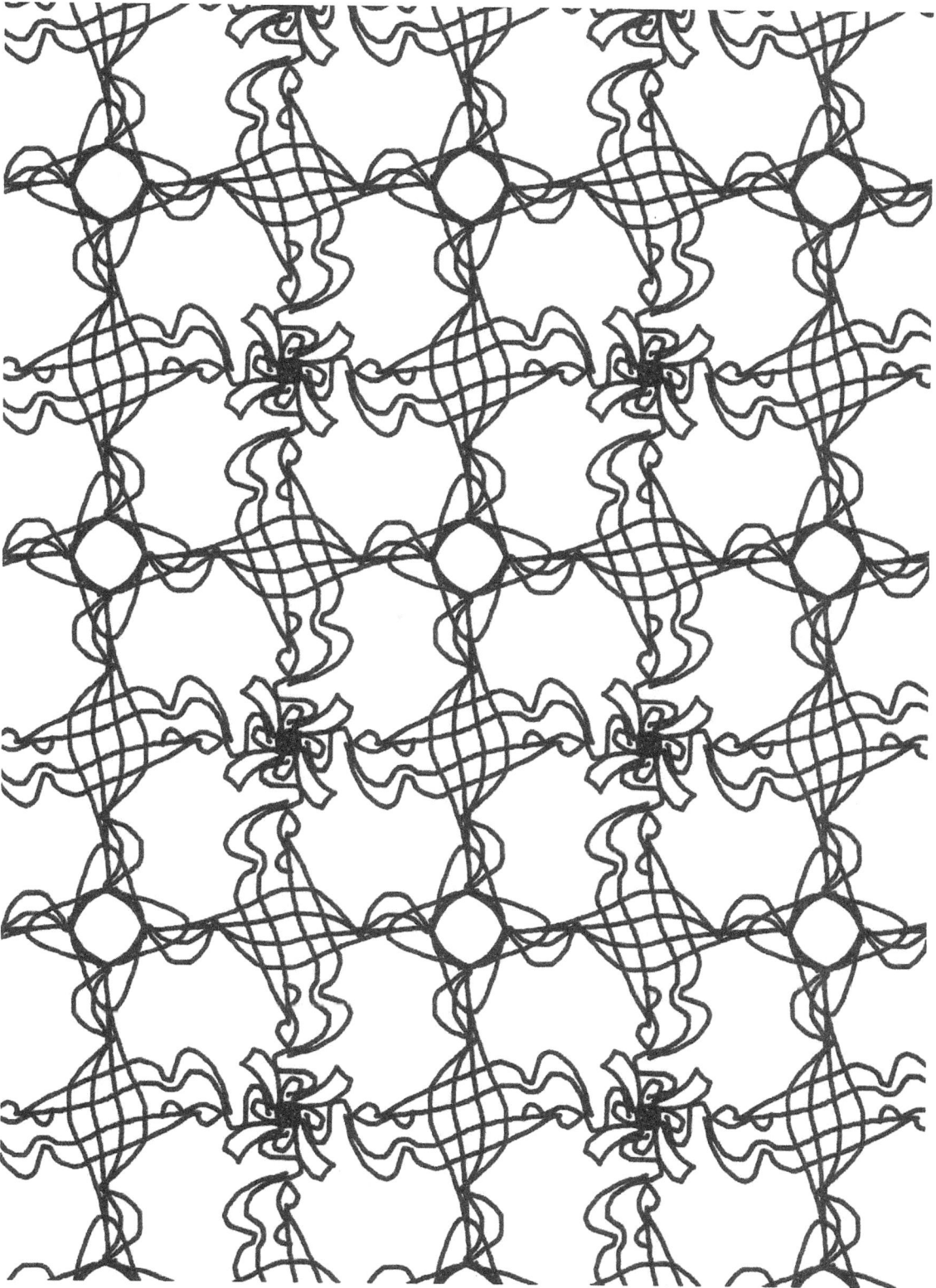

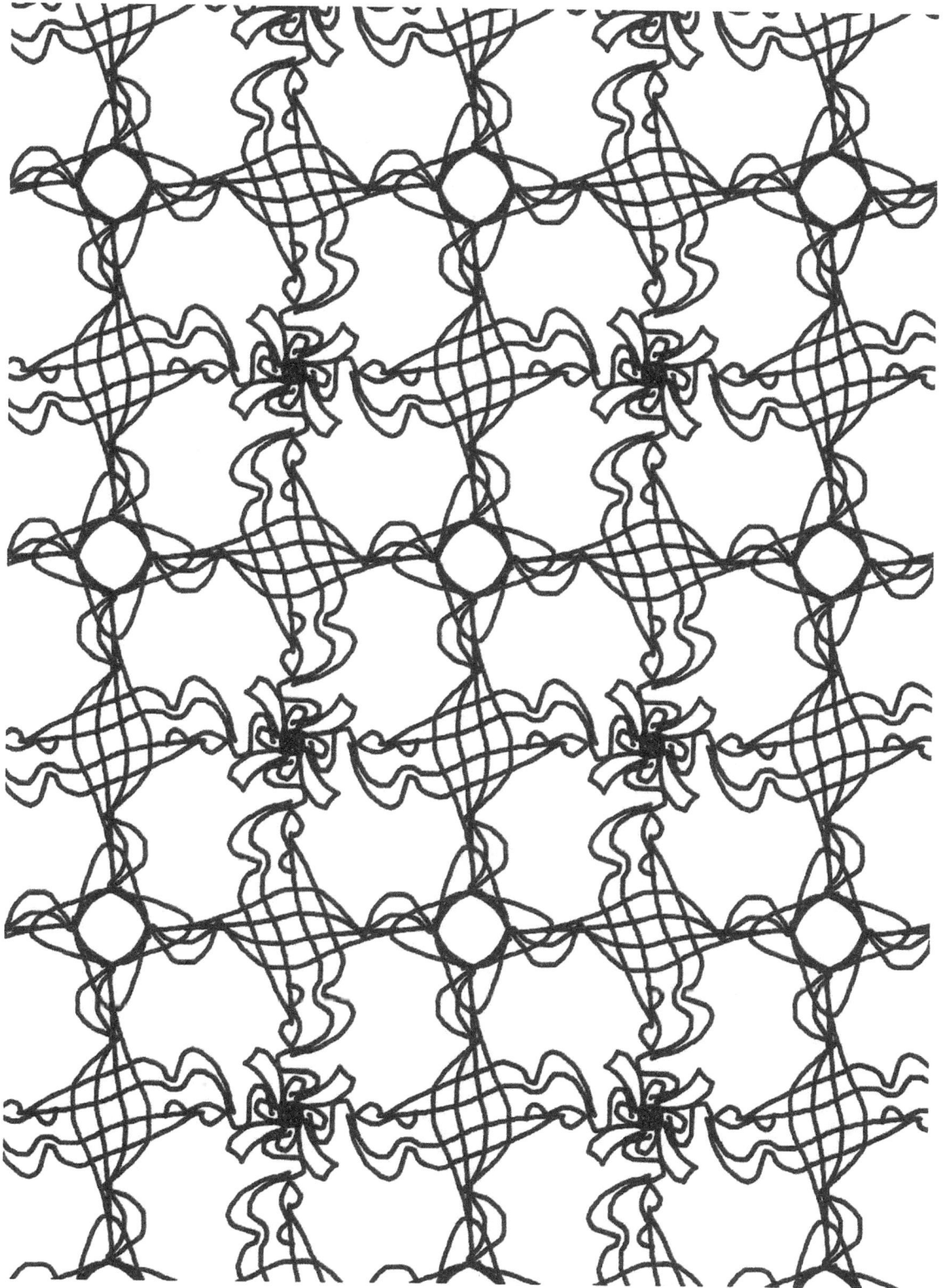

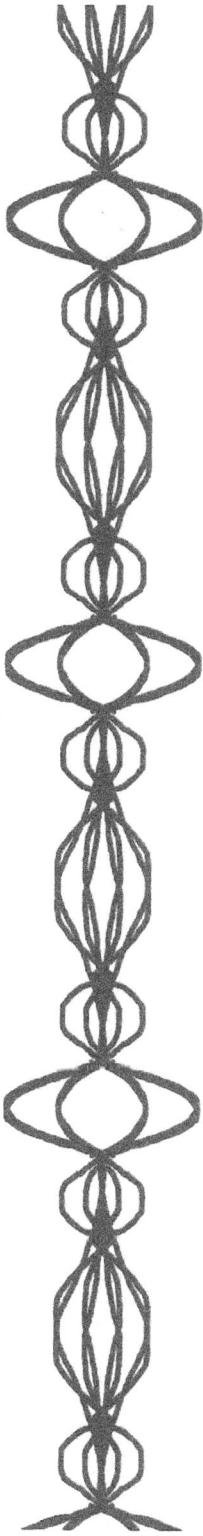

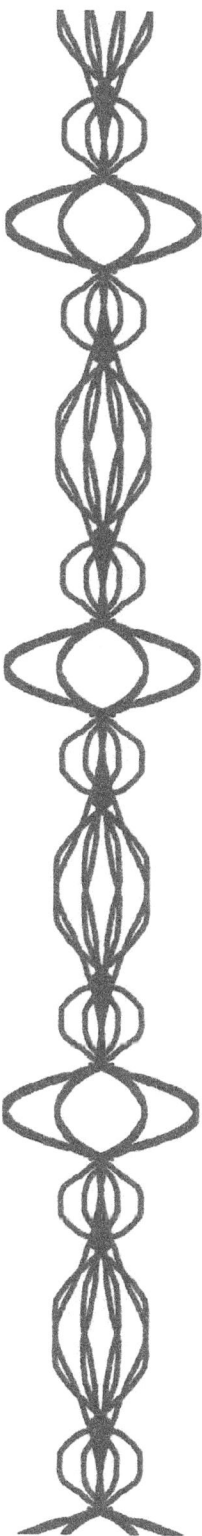

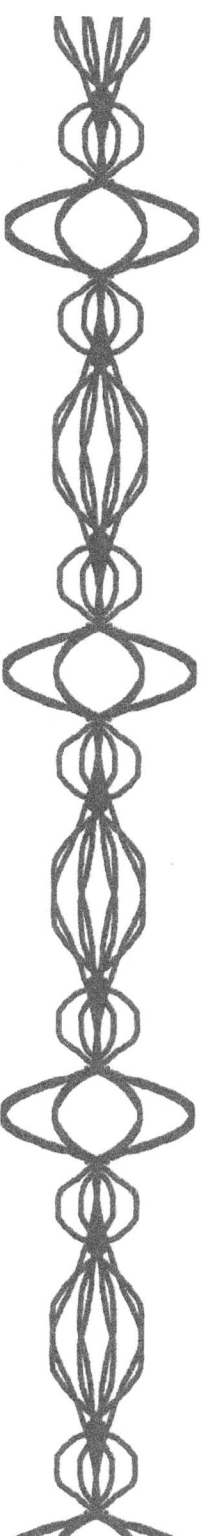

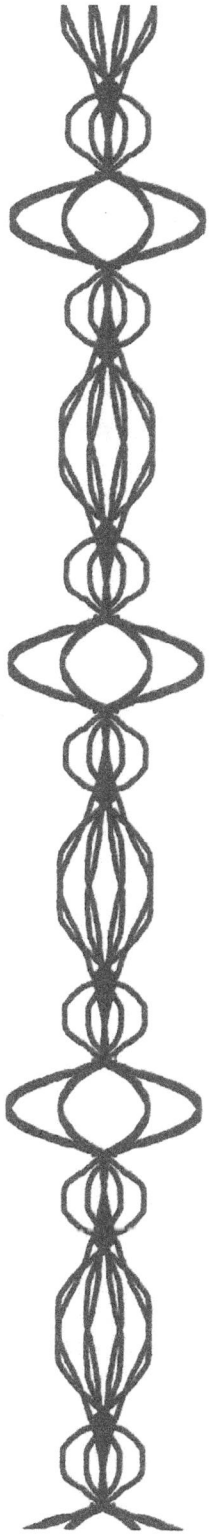

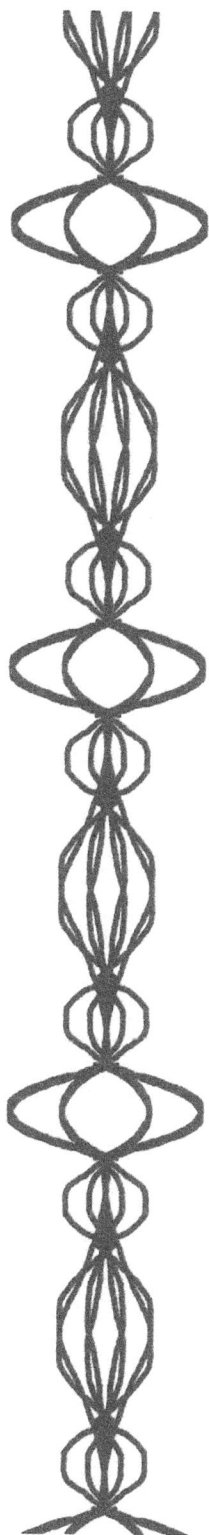

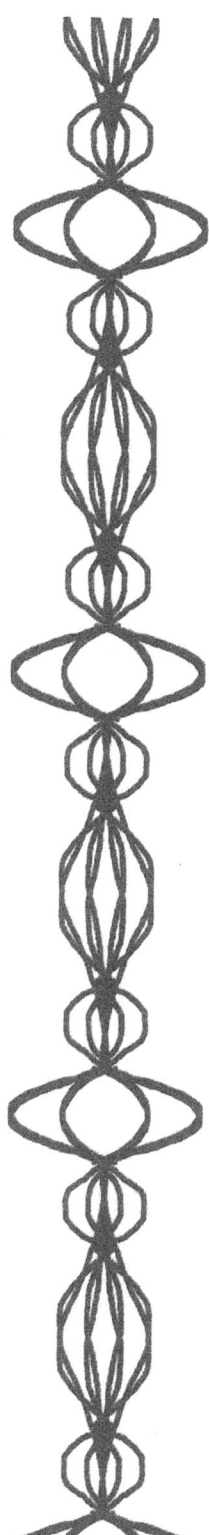

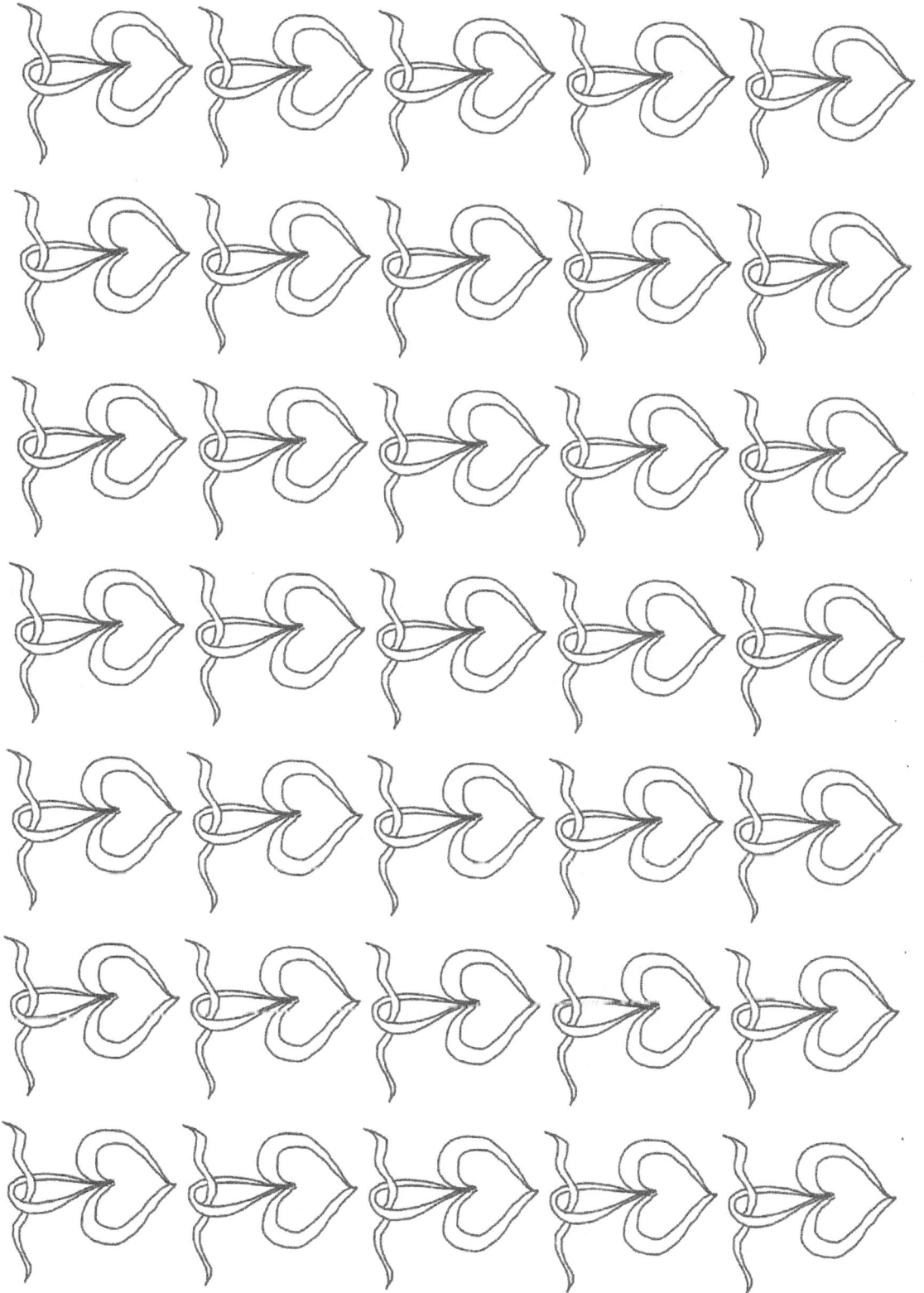

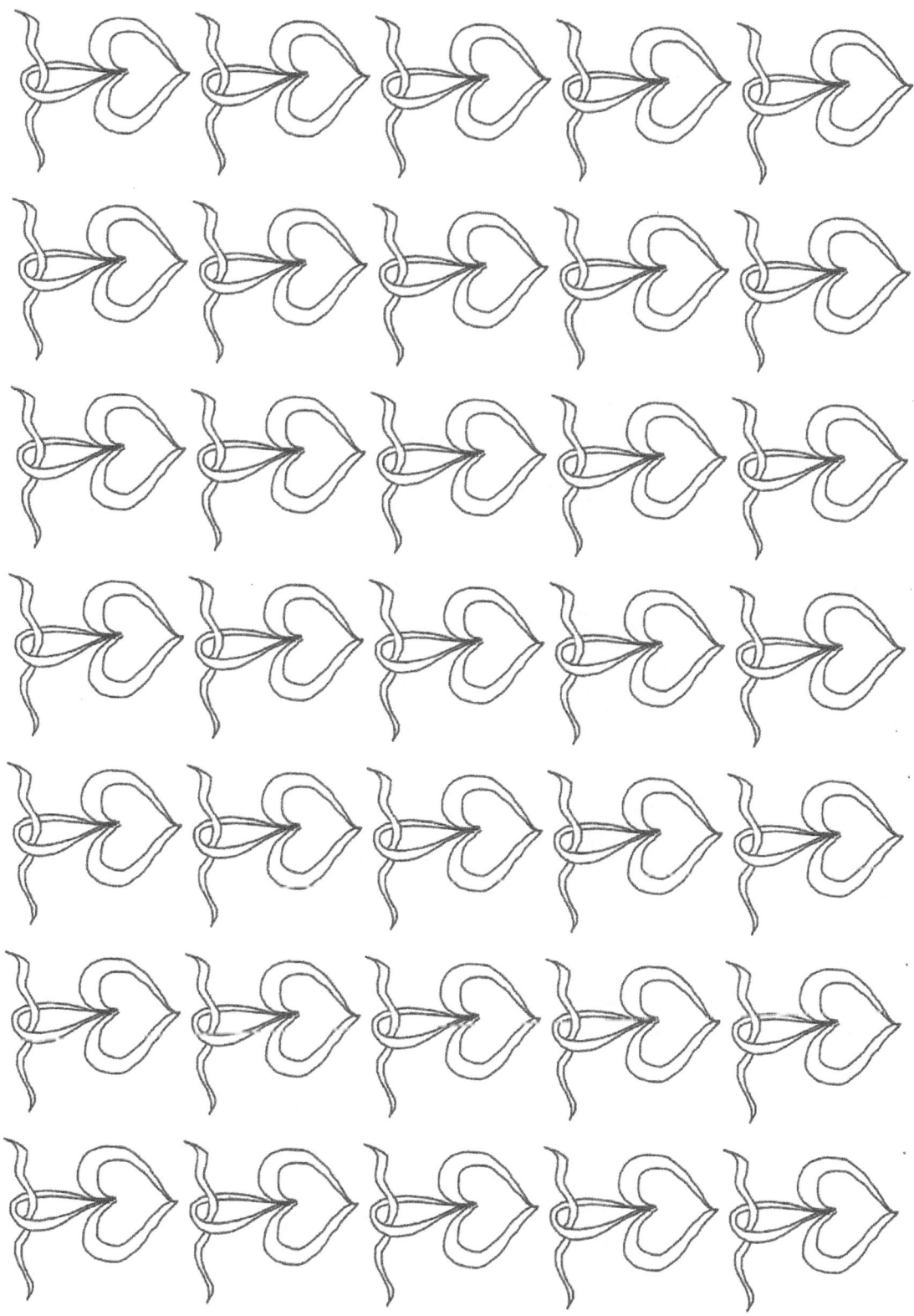

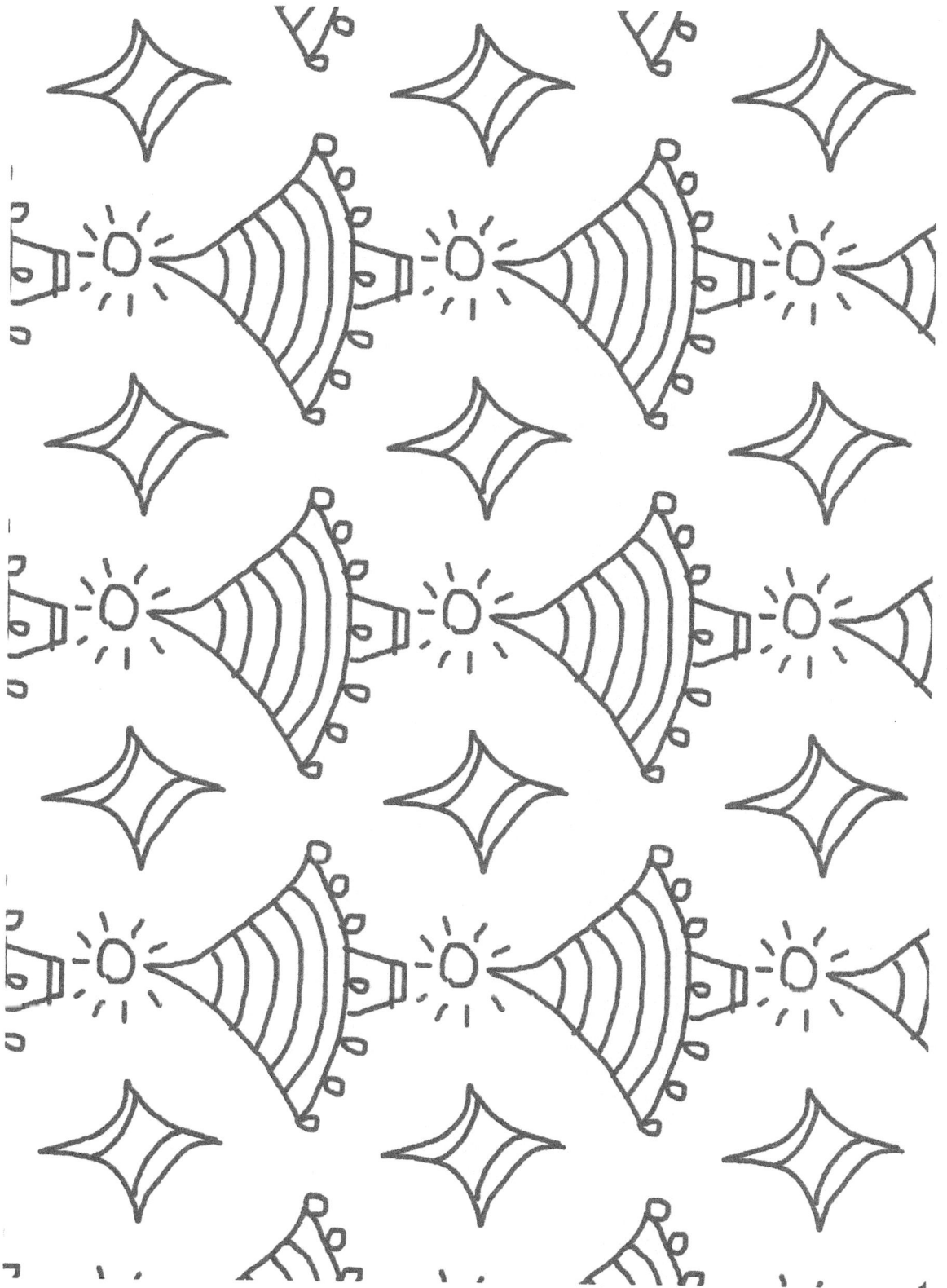

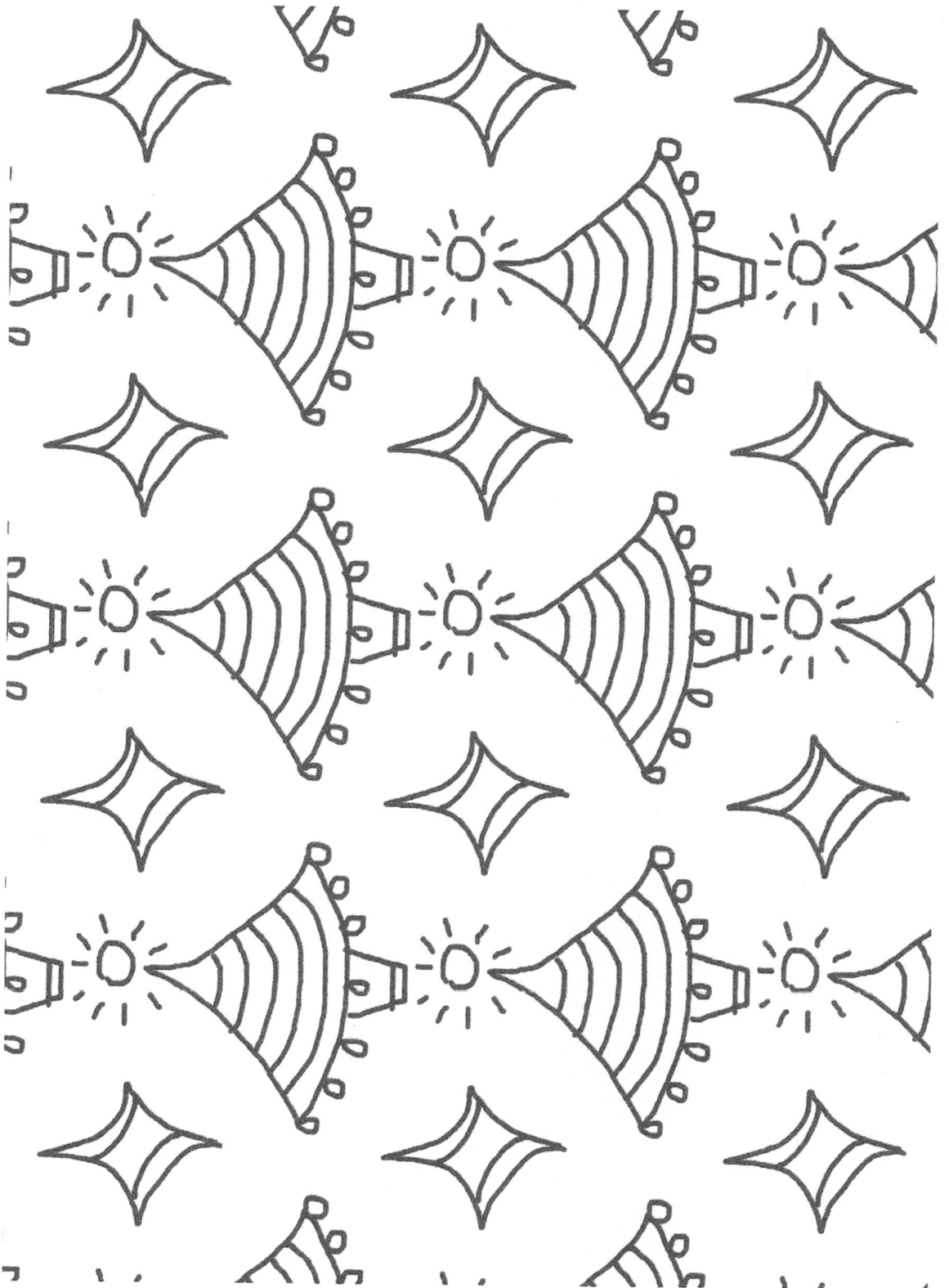

USING INK?

Tear out any of these extra pages, and
place them behind the page you're coloring
to protect the following pages from any ink overflow.

Or, you can use these pages as book markers,
to write a list of pencils you need,
or mess around with color combinations.

Enjoy coloring!

Peace to you and yours.

USING INK?

Tear out any of these extra pages, and
place them behind the page you're coloring
to protect the following pages from any ink overflow.

Coloring can be a very relaxing and quite absorbing pastime.
Don't forget to take a little break, have a snack and
something to drink once in a while!

Coloring Camelot

Be sure to visit our Facebook page,
"Coloring Camelot Adventures,"
where free downloads are often found
as well as the occasional raffle for lovely prizes!

In addition to this coloring book, you can find
others by Suzanna Stinnett on Amazon.

Look for **"Christmas Coloring Fun for All"** for
more classical scenes and wrapping paper fun,
"Hidden Realms Within" for unusual designs
that can take you on a personal journey,
and **"Color Puzzles,"** a book with heavy black designs
in tile shape and a mathematical style,
for colorers ready for a challenge.

www.ingramcontent.com/pod-product-compliance
Lightning Source LLC
Chambersburg PA
CBHW080520030426
42337CB00023B/4583